Scars/Stars

Walidah Imarisha

Drapetomedia

Portland, Oregon

1 2 3 4 5 6 7 8 9 10

FIRST EDITION
October 2013

Published by Walidah Imarisha
in conjunction with Drapetomedia, LLC.
Portland, OR 97213
www.walidah.com

Library of Congress Control Number:
2013944347

ISBN-10: 0983355738
ISBN-13: 978-0-9833557-3-1

Portions of this book have appeared in other collections, periodicals,
and websites.

Cover design by Vagabond
Interior design by David Walker

To my mother, who shows me what a true love of words and an unbreakable spirit look like everyday.

Table of Contents

Lessons

it is time now
to call the children
in from the dusky brilliance of the street light
              line them like *matyoshka* dolls
on the living room carpet
teach them the truth
                       of blood
smeared sticky across the face of night

Second Chances

You
my ex partner
my sometimes lover
my always love
are beautiful

I am in the midst of death
but that is just the way
amerika
smells
on a hot texas day

And I have to write this
to honor
a warrior
If death row
can't slice up a sacred heart
then I
have a lot of blood
to start pumping

Touched my face
with willow tree fingers
said

>   *Look*
>   *a butterfly*
>   *just flew*
>   *from your eye*
>   *landed on your left cheek*

There are no third chances
with courts or *compas*

Sanctuary

Trust me
I trusted you
I know how ugly/beautiful you are
I have seen your scars
I have kissed all your scars

Even our scars
are beautiful

And we
none of us
not a one

We
will not be
washed away

Wade in the Water

I.
There was still water
standing
6 feet deep
in people's homes
two weeks after the flood.

Through waters laced
with chemicals
and human excrement
and bloated bodies,
Black and brown people
went out everyday
to save the kin
left behind.

King George said,
"Let them eat flood water!"
They choked
on the watery debris
called progress.

"Please,"
he said
standing in a small canoe
floating in what remained
of the 7th Ward
hands in the air
eyes trained on the hypnotic guns
of 3 officers
who minutes before had
fired 4 shots
that may or may not
have been warnings.

"Please,"
he said
heart heavy in his mouth,
"I am looking for the body of my son -
Let me find my son's body."

II.
The Mississippi River
was dragged in the 1960s to find
the bodies of three civil rights workers
murdered by the klan.
Dozens of human remains were found
all Black   all nameless.
They were unimportant
to officials and bureaucracy
and media coverage
and "good" race relations
so they were thrown back
to the river.

How many lives were submerged
until they stopped
kicking?

The Mississippi is claiming
the bodies of the lynched
once again.

III.
Muddied rings still stain
the waists of houses.
Bodies of rotting dogs
congeal
in the stilted Louisiana sun.
In a town an hour outside of New Orleans
corpses were unearthed

from their graves,
set free to float down the street.
An old man sits on his porch.
"I built this house
with my hands.
Lived here 58 years
with my wife -
'til she died two years ago.
I saw her casket
in the waters
two weeks ago.
No one will help me
put her back in the ground
so she can rest.
                    Won't anyone help me?"

IV.
DEARGOD PleASE HELP US
FEMA
dONT LeAVE US TO dIE
read the graffiti on a house
completely surrounded
by water

Two weeks and no relief
Three weeks and no aid
Four weeks and no FEMA

"Yeah, they gave us sumthin,"
the brotha snorted
dreads coiled and purring on his head.
He was one in boats
Every day
taking people to the promised land
of higher ground.
"On the 5th day

Red Cross
dropped some hard rock candy
on our heads.
Don't let them tell you
they never gave us nuthin."

They gave them
National Guard
and NYPD
and INS and Border Patrol
and the Office of Homeland Security
and state troopers and US Marshalls
and the DEA and corrections officers
and detachments and battalions
and tanks
and automatic weapons and Hummers
and curfew and work camps
and concrete floors
and nightsticks
and blood
and bullets

Don't let them tell you
they never gave us
nuthin.

V.
The water recedes.
The human tide
trickles in.
An oldyoung woman
stands in her decomposing house,
black mold climbing up the walls,
coating baby pictures
and high school diplomas.
Her 4 daughters

chase after their 11 collective children.
She holds the youngest in her arms
and he is nothing
but wise eyes and heavy brow.
"Of course we stayin,"
she hefts the tiny sage to the other hip.
"I don't know what we gonna do…
But this
is ours.
We won't leave it."

She does not mean the cramped house
and dead yard out front.
She means this spark of hope
soggy
sputtering
but burning out
enough space
to catch a breath.

Communion

the boy next to me on the bus
listening to
wu-tang
on his ipod
is
praying…

eyes closed
lips moving
silent incantations:

> *hip hop is my life, son*
> *it's a religion*

i want to shake him
until his crown of cornrows flies free
and ask him
what he hears
when he communes with
gods

Head Voice Father My My

in memory of my father

She does look like me.
Long tall drink of water,
Legs and fingers
That seem to never end.
I didn't know what to expect
Pacing Grip's porch
At 9 p.m.
Puffing my fifth cigarette in
20 minutes.
They were four hours late,
And I thought
Maybe they changed
Their mind.
Maybe they weren't coming.
Maybe it was a joke that ole Grip
Played on me,
And it would be something she'd do
Cause she never took to me
Dating her best friend
And I guess I can understand that.
Now.

Then the car pulled up,
And they got out:
My ex wife
Heavier
Older
But still just as beautiful
As the last day I saw her.
This time
There were no tears
Marring her face.

Then out stepped
A vision of me.
All that mess of hair
And curt motions.
My child.
Youngest of seven.
Last I saw her
She was four
And talking up a storm.
"Read me Cindegrella
Daddy
Read me Cindegrella
Again"
As she pulled the orange ET doll
I gave her tight
And looked at me with
Broken guitar string eyes.
Her eyes
Just the same
Now
23 years later.
They locked on me
And made me feel
All those years of running
And Lord,
I am tired.

Took her to the park the next day
To talk.
Stopped to get me a beer on the way
At Sam's little corner store.
I asked her if she thought I was an alcoholic.
She said no.
She lied.

Full of spit and fire,
Those eyes
Never left me as she asked
Everything under the hot Mississippi sun:
Why did I leave them
And
Did I miss them
And
How many children do I have
And
Where do my people come from
And what was it like
Dating a white women in the 70s...
I tried to give her answers -
It was the least she deserved
And the most I could give.

She showed me all the things she'd done
Movies and books and songs
And poems and stuff like that,
And I was so proud of this daughter,
This stranger,
Standing in front of me.

I wanted to stay longer
But the longer I stayed
The harder it was to leave.

I felt the years pressing down on me
And I didn't want
To cry in front of my baby.
Not yet
Anyway.

I sat down
When I got back to this one room

I call all mine
Pulled out my guitar
Played a song
I wrote for her
When she was seven
And far from me.
She's never heard it.

I wonder
If she's ever gonna
Put me
In a poem?

Broken

I am
Broken
And no one will
Play
With me
For fear
Of cutting themselves
On my sharp
Edges.

Masterpiece

"When I die
I wear nothing but the tats on my back"
- Kakamia Jahad Imarisha

His body
Tapestry
Memory
Masterpiece
Writing his name on the sun
                    His skin
Roadmap of ink and flesh
The raised Braille of keloid scars

Mouth full of broken angel wings
And arm full of India ink rage
Injected by a prison gun
In bold styles
No one could ignore
Ivy letters crept up his neck

The cynicism of
Fuck the World
In bold Olde English letters
African warrior
Shield and spear in hand
Rises sphinx-like from the small of his back
Shadowed by a one foot anarchy symbol
Thug scholar to ruffneck revolutionary
Machetero symbols
Kamikaze graffiti
And a fucked up picture of Da Brat
From when he was 15

And no box can hold him

Doctors told him to lay off the toxins
They cut out the cancer
Located directly under his right nipple
Two inch wound
Camouflaged by the symbol for
Eternal energy

He paints his scars brightly
In defiance of death
Mocks the Grim Reaper
By taking his name
Draws a bulls eye in the middle
Of his chest
With the edict
No warning shots

His whole life
Has been a carcinogen

My adopted brother
Living memorial
Walking Vietnam Wall
A place people go
To remember atrocities
To mourn lost loved ones
To pray for forgiveness
To vow
Never
Again
Victoria
Jackie Jr.
Thearon
Dice
Qui-Que
A litany of those
Who slipped through fingers

Outstretched through bars
Dead partnas
And momma
Sons
Brothers
Cousins
All on his body
He walks with the weight
Of exquisite corpses
His footsteps
Echo tenfold
For the multitudes
Who live
On his skin

He carries a picture of me
Embedded over his heart
We breath as one
His name soaked into my wrist
Pulsing with my pulse
We inject our familial bonds
Umbilical cord needle
Blood clots
Tender flesh
Joined by more than
Blood or ink

Lost

I wandered lost
in the concrete desert
for four centuries.

I passed jesus in his manger
      an afroed baby
         with thug in his eye

and lips too big
to be of anything
but god.

Stayed

I.
Never scared of the dark

Never turned my face away
On the street
2 am walks through cityscapes
Looked dead into the faces of strangers
And smiled

I have never been hurt by strangers
Only lovers
Lovers of freedom
Justice
Righteousness
Lovers? of me

II.
Scared in my skin
Scared of your touch
Which will take too much of me
You ask for a sip
       Instead up end me
Until my muffled sobs
Trail down your chin

III.
I stayed
In your arms
Trying to scrape the last taste
Of comfort
From the roof of my mouth

IV.
Well if she stayed

It wasn't isn't won't be so bad
None of our
I mean it's really just hers
And she really is just his
Their personalispolitical business

V.
Why do so many of us
Have green eyes?
Not for love
        Only because of love

VI.
Gurl I tole ya
Well maybe you shouldna
Have been
Wit that white boy in the first place
        Second class
Last place
Shoulda known better
Cuz we taught you better

                Whose hands
                Are around
                My throat

I thought I knew

VII.
A word
On influencing people
And winning friends
Always be pleasant
Polite
Ready with a smile
Ask neutral questions

That leave room for
Civil discussion
Avoid controversial topics
At all cost

VIII.
Gogoinggonewent

IX.
Held breath
Echoing pulse
Dead universe
Silent womb
What is left
Of pride
Where do I buy
Second-hand forgiveness
When I'm not even sure I need it
  Gift wrap it
  Or can I wear it out of the store
Better safe
Than sorry

X.
I must find a way
To live
In this flesh

Shattered Haiku

He shattered my thighs
I rain down his cheeks and streak
Cum/tears/rainwater

My Love for You

the abortion
Was
Three weeks
Ago.

expect bleeding
They said
For 2-6 weeks.

sometimes
The flow
Lightens
Gradually

then in a torrent
Blood soaks
Through everything.

i will continue
To bleed
Until I am myself
Again.

Scars

Don't ask about my scars
Just don't cause any new ones

They Deported My Love Last Night

They arrested my heart last night.
I tried to secret it away
but they traced it with
satellite systems
bloodhounds
motion detectors.

They tracked it by
the smell of rebirth.

They disappeared my passion last night.
Without warning
burst into the bedroom
left only
a rapidly cooling
yawning void
in our bed.

They detained
searched
interrogated my hope
last night
fired innuendos
spit lewd suggestions.

They strip-searched my faith.

They brutalized and beat my dreams
for not denouncing me.
With hot pokers and plungers
mace handcuffs electrodes
broken broom handles batons bats
fire hoses rope fists malice
they tried to twist my joy

into something they could control.
And when that did not work
they deported my love
last night.

Blood Wails

"Time of death is 6:15 pm."
The warden's metallic voice
warbles through the plexiglass casket
Sobs of family members
scratch the silence
The victim's family
is the held breath of intermission
Red curtain jerks closed

The hood is hot
It grates the back of my neck
The acidic afterburp of over sugared coffee
gurgles at the back of my throat
as I slide the needle into a vein
Arms outstretched metal gurney crucifixion
Eyes that serenade me
with the softness of Jake's
when he was a newborn
I feel bile in my throat

The body is heavy
Frank and Jim grunt
as they lift the shell
The cords in my neck
contract
Out of the corner of my eye
I watch them dance the corpse
out of the room
I think of long ago
of Jillian's warm hands
plucking notes
from the small of my back
The coils of her climax wrapped tight

The night is dark
as I slip out of the prison
The lights from candles
eyes wide open
The symphony of signs
I don't bother to read anymore
for
against
The faces are all the same refrain

The drive is long
an hour infinite
I don't turn on the music
I don't want to feel it on my flesh
This
This is the hardest part
The needle stabs 90
smell of burnt rubber

The house is deathly silent
keys on the coffee table a high hat
naked feet on carpet a muted drum
Each step a climbing crescendo
creaking bedroom door
pants slap floor
heavy with wallet
sharp hiss of bed springs
sad sigh of down comforter
The pills in my hand
a series of dropped notes
I stopped counting them out
years ago

Jillian's body punctures
the opera with silence
The cacophony of that day

every day
lies cut and bleeding
She is awake
She is always awake
unforgiving
unmoving
The body
cooling in the funeral home
draped in the cheapest suit
no shoes
No one ever lifts
a casket lid

I will dream
as always
The needle's nose dive
Veins of fire
My ears stuffed full
of voices
lives that were
smoldering candle wicks
between my fingers
I know
I know
it will never stop
As sleep claws
at me,
Jillian snorts,
turns her face
to the blank wall

We end the night
as we end every night
With the wail of blood
between us

Breathing Bomb

"It was what she had battling inside her.
An unmixable mix.
The infinite tenderness of motherhood
and the reckless rage of a suicide bomber."
 –Arundhati Roy, *The God of Small Things*

black helicopters heralded my arrival,
ghetto birds pecking at the slums
ushered in my birth.

I came out my momma
with eyes full of tenements
and penitentiaries.
born without lids
I saw
my mother's screams embedded
into project walls.
that's the last time
I saw her cry.

sometimes ma would look at me,
mouth full of ash:
 "shit, whose kid are you?"
her lips stained black and worn down flat.
"whose bastard mule-atto mixed up
unclaimed tainted forgotten bruised kid
are you, anyway?"

pop was a vietnam vet
fighting a daily war
as unwinnable and unpopular
as the one in the 'nam.
washed away the taste of napalm,

taking that night train
until one day,
he forgot how to come home.
agent orange cold war madness
jungle rot in my genes,
straight no chaser
until I strangle on my own cells.

so I encased and sealed my feet
in combat boots,
when I was in the white man's uniform
in foreign lands
and nothing felt like home,
ya dig?
children play war
swaddled in govt. issued fatigues.

I leak at the seams
overflow like a stopped up sewer drain.
I can't live without blood on my hands
and I could give a fuck whose it is.

bombed out buildings
inside
brown men and women
crack apart
leave nothing but glass vials
and burnt spoons.

sirens
always
in my dreams
in my nightmares
even in the womb.
it echoes
in the pounding of my chest.

sucked up by
slum streets and ghetto gaza strips
where I had more than rocks
and less than rage
to fuel me.
14 years old
breaking and entering
my first offense -
other than my birth.
judge gave me a three year bid.
you goin call me a thief, man?
you listen to elvis,
muthafucka.

tagged up cells
walls
eternity
scratched my name on buildings
and in the train yards
before they had them new trains
and I didn't give a shit who went over it --
it was just my blood on those walls.

had a lover once
soul clear as rainwater
we exchanged needles like kisses.
the only beautiful thang
I had to give.

I used to dance to my uncle's
salsa and soul records,
hips crashing like congas,
practiced moves on rusty fire escapes
and project rooftops,
pigeons my only audience.

more *bomba* than bomb
but it bes that way sometimes.

in a time punctured by machetes,
i coulda been the grandchild of che.
you know people tell me
i kinda look like him.
or assata.
they say i look like her too...

maybe it's the guns.

but this is a time of
cracked and splintered eyes
and my insides
are ticking a countdown.

what's that sound?
just the blowback,
and you're standing
right in the way
of the firewall.

Poetry

Poetry don't live in ivory towers
Wrapped in mink
Wiping its ass on silk
And farting Pulitzer prizes

Poetry gets down and dirty
Cuz it's got nowhere else to go
Poetry bleeds breathes
With scraped and bruised knuckles
A broken nose
And Poetry won't tell you who did it
Poetry knows how to take care of itself

Poetry pops pills and shoots up
Slippery with mucus and vomit
With faded burn scars
Hidden questions in the ER at 2 am
Poetry is placed in foster homes
Pregnant and alone
It avoids eye contact with others
Hides its face from jagged mirror edges
It writes its name on walls
In marker acrylic aerosol
Spray paint shit blood
Than erases it so no knows
Poetry is afraid
Of its own distorted face

Poetry mumbles to itself on street corners
Urinates in hallways
Puts its fist through stubborn walls
Poetry is under psychiatric evaluation
To monitor its ability
To understand reality

Poetry is what people
Cross the street to avoid

Disowned
Divorced
Disregarded
It lashes out
Poetry hurts the ones it loves

In a cold sweat
Haunted by nightmares
Poetry gets the shakes
Poetry would rather forget
Swigs hard liquor
Snorts dust
Turns into dust
Poetry licks wounds and lines

Sometimes Poetry
Doesn't even
Understand
Itself

Rope burns around its neck
Poetry straps a bomb to its chest
And walks into the courthouse
Liberates its comrades from behind unjust walls
Doesn't look into the faces
Of children playing across the street
Before it pushes the detonator

Poetry kills
Packs heat
And Poetry remembers
Pulling the trigger

With a bandolier bracelet
And dirty hands
Poetry talks down suicide jumpers
Poetry has never felt loved
Has felt a marine's bullet
Tear through flesh
The impact of nightstick
And pavement
Married as one

Poetry saves lives
And slits its own wrists
And Poetry wants to live

Poetry has tubes up its nose
Morphin drip
Pumped stomach
Bandaged head
And doctors
That say
The AZT seems to be having no effect

Poetry coughs up bloody bile
The experts say
Poetry is dying

Poetry is not dead yet

In fact, Poetry thinks it will live
Forever
Spitting poison
Dancing on the ashes of civilization
Stuck between the sky and the earth
It stands in the spotlight
Defies any judgment
Especially its own

Poetry is learning to forgive itself
Poetry is trying to love itself
And Poetry loves you
More than you love
Your own goddamned self

Vulcanization

I live out my nightmares
Re-enact them in the crunch
Of my nails
On flesh
I have tried to tear
This caul from my face
Until my skin peeled
Back

I cannot escape my flesh
Used and useless
Hurt and humming
Burned   Battered
The head
Of a drum
The hands of a master

This is just the echo
Of the last note
Struck
I will be the silence
In between notes
Again
That's where the music
Lives
That's where the light
Cracks
Thru
This perfect offering

I will live in this flesh
Without regards to the
Pitchforks
And burning torches

The villagers carry
The smell of sulfur
No longer disturbs me
This is where the strongest
Alloy is forged

This is my vulcanization process
Baby
And I am honored to stand
In the presence of
Noble and notable
Niggas
Such as yourselves.

My Cunt Smells

My cunt smells
Of sulfur and **ash**
Echoes of what burned there

Tagging

"shit, you gotta tag trains"
he said, twirling a spray paint can
like a six shooter.
"yo, walls are nice and all,
but how else people
as far as st. louis and cali
goin see your name?
now that's immortality."

train tracks crisscross this country
like the river lethe
where truth is
what is remembered,
embedded into the soil
and into our minds
into our history
as mighty engines rumble over
uneasingly sleeping ground.

outlaws used to rob trains,
conquering this symbol
of civilization's expanding force
which had carried them to the west,
like unwanted children.
They were vomited
onto unfamiliar ground,
only to return
in a prodigal blaze of bullets
and perform manifest destiny
on the cargo sleeping in its belly,
where they had refused to sleep.

one graf artist said
"i can't afford no billboards,

this is my billboard."
one slave said
"here is your freedom,"
holding aloft a gun.
others preferred to make their voices heard
through the soles of their feet
rather than the barrels of rifles.
their feet
transformed into wheels
as they rumbled through
the underground railroad
liberating property
not as outlaws
but as contraband.

they stole themselves
in plantation hold-ups.

and wasn't john henry
trying to hold up progress
when this big ole black man
challenged a train to a duel?

they had to use that
steam-powered powerful engine
to push his dead body
off the tracks
he laid
with his two
slave
hands.

they dumped his body
on the side of the road,
imported exploited asian labor
to drive rails into his still warm shell,

the blood from his burst heart
seeping into the ground,
mixing with the culture and screams
of stolen land
stolen red land
while chinese exclusion laws
were forced to build
the industrial revolution
on john henry's corpse.

trains rode over him until he disappeared,
became a breathing part of the earth
rails expanding like lungs,
breathing out locomotive trains

which during the depression
transported hoboes
from one end of the country to the other,
in a period where times
were hard for everyone…
and a whole lot harder for some.
ask the scottsboro boys
or at least the one remaining
because when
these young black men
tried to ride the rails
to escape crushing southern poverty
and sharecropping destinies,
they found themselves
at the end of a
courtroom noose.

freedom of movement
comes with a price
for those who are still
contraband

just as spray paint cans
are contraband
in a place with no free walls,
only blank walls,
only prison walls

so static and lifeless you long to see paint
and words and pictures fly by in a blur
you long to see yourself fly by in a blur,
embedded into box cars
coloring the countryside
at every stop,
dripping pieces of sweat and fear and pride
onto the blood-soaked stolen land
where once outlaws dared to defy
the unquestioned faceless authority
of the train tracks,
which cut this nation like a surgeon's blade.
just as nightly train yards are defiled
by voices screaming to be heard
from tags rumbling
across the country
etched into the side of
manifest destiny

now that's

immortality.

Graf Kid

His heart
Rests
In his back pocket
Next to his Krylon
Can
He cannot commit
To anything
Lasting longer
Than one tip
I watch him
Blur by
Trying to read him
Like throw ups
On the side
Of a moving train

My Left Eye

do not love too big
your heart squeezed between
fragile eggshells of ribs
keep it small enough
to hold in one cupped hand
protected by jagged wings
do not let it flavor
your tongue
saturate your spit
until it glistens like dew
keep love
tucked in your cheek
confined
controlled

I have been battered
to my roots
by the ravages of my own heart
I have showered myself
upon another's head
slid down his upturned
moon face
pooled
at the corners of his lips
shaped like Africa

the brilliance of a sun
can suck dry
any land
and he burned hotter
than redemption
building his house
of whitened bone
scorched blood

and chaste hope
I found myself alone
with only the darkness
licking
my ear
my endless love
slowly crushing
my handmade temple

learn to only love small
I told my aching flesh
I will love this rock
and that fingernail
I will love the word sacrament
and I will love that window pane
I will love the color maroon
my left eye my wool sweater
this patch of concrete the month of March
the number 12
I will love things I can count
and mark
and touch
I will love people only in safe doses
holding them lightly
prepared to let go
letting go first
so I will not be left
with my broken wings
wrapped tight

I will not rest myself
in someone else's heart
having the audacity to think
I could spread out
drape my clothes on arteries
hang my family picture on a vein

and fall asleep
to the warm sound of
blood
singing

I will live in my own skin
I will hide in my own skin
I will die in my own skin

my face sheltered so long
I forgot
I exist beyond the color
of mere existence
the pain of fingers
poking old rages
and the shadow
of his contradictions

I peel back the slopes
of my face
take in the gravity
of my thighs
the way my eyes
milk
the sky for laughter
I want to open my arms
gather
my never were/might be children
together
raise them up
the light
reflecting off their mirrored flesh
I will see a thousand mes
broken and birthed
whole and healing
fractured and fiery

I will unpeel my fist
just a little more
each morning

I will hear
the soft beating
of wings

Love in the Trenches

He is a Technicolor bright red star
On a titled beret
Black
As revolution

She is an afro on a wanted poster
Clear eyes staring out
And scaring the shit
Out of those who ain't
Got a clue

He is a black mask on the face
Of a child who has had enough
Of the tanks and checkpoints

She is hands
Around a shocked soldier's throat
As the crowd surges forward
Overpowering rifles and
Gas canisters with the sheer force of
Flesh

He is birthright reclaimed upraised
Fist clutching a gun on the
Top of the city's capitol building

She is a Molotov cocktail
Thrown suspended midair flames
Licking the sky ready
To kiss the earth

He is recovered plans to government
Facilities and she is the bomb
He lays

She is a safe house offered
By a 65 year old grandmother
He is donations from a check stretched
Paper thin to feed a family of six
Because they believe in
Her and him

She is lined up against the wall
Government guns trained on her while
She yells "don't mourn, organize"

He is rapid-fire grenade detonation
Artillery napalm bomb lullabies

She is atrocities committed covered
In blood so that children may sleep
Through the night in peace

He is whispered *"para la
Revolucion"* as he kisses his newborn
Daughter's tiny hand

He is food smuggled into the hole for
A political prisoner
And she is guns smuggled into
Occupied territory

She is an uprising he is a
Rebellion she is an
Insurrection he is a
Manifesto she is a
Communiqué he is a
Free school she is a
Political education
Class he is a
Kiss she is an

Embrace they are
Whispers in the
Heart of the people they are
Love in the trenches

Minefields

I slept in a minefield
Unexploded devices as my pillow
A blanket of explosives snuggled tight
My eyes scream faster than light
There is no REM beneath my lids
Just bombs and bombs and
Concrete cushions for my head
Urban decay the horizon
Two babies strapped to my back
Doze on the subway
One eye open
To ward off roaming hands
Chase the dreams away

One moment of reverie
Can cost you
Everything

I used to daydream on the El
Shadows dancing across
Scratched up plexiglass
My baby's wail a
Six part opera
The conductor's voice
        More scarred than the plexiglass
Angels
Reading heavenly forecasts

My mind was pinwheels
Starbursts galactic light shows
My head housed escape
My body lived
In the cracks of the sidewalk
My tongue

Coated with toxin
I carried a refuge
Inside me
I slept through the night
In peace
Stray bullets brushed my cheeks
I did not stir
C4 canisters rapped on my window
I stretched and rolled over

Zyklon gas
Slowly leaked under the door
Snuck up my nose
On a night
I got caught sleeping
On that long ride
  As Mikey said
Uptown
Downtown
Crosstown
I woke to
More pieces of me
Dead
Spiritual leprosy
Bandits marauding
Stole bits of my sunshine
The fog rolled in
  I learned to breath in
The fumes
Without chokingblinkingthinking
I dropped to earth
Landed in this flesh
My tomb
  Here
Without visions
To haunt my indecisions

My disappointments
Bombed out housing
And military patrols
And choked screams
And random checkpoints
And hungry eyes
Are the familiar

It is not pretty

And neither am I

Military Targets

They say
they only bomb military targets.
Only military targets
they coo soothingly.
We are not terrorists,
setting bombs
and stealing planes
and stabbing at the night
which asphyxiates and poisons.
We have clean shirts
and clean hands
and we sterilize our instruments
before we operate.

Israeli soldiers
invaded Ramallah today.
I only know this
because a white activist
told me so.
He said
>Israeli soldiers invaded Ramallah today
>and I am so depressed,
>I can't go out to dinner with you guys.
He would rather sit
in silent contemplation
of a Jack Daniels bottle.
I told him to remember to
pour out a little liquor
for our Palestinian homies.

He told me
my humor
at a time like this
was inappropriate.

Liberals shake their heads
and from towers of privilege
cluck the appropriate nothings
that run from their lips
like diarrhea:
> *It is so sad*
> *It is a tragedy*
> *There must be peace*
> *We must stop the violence*
> *in the Middle East!*
Which rose from…?
Nowhere
like a mushroom cloud
without memory
no culpability   no anger
only depression.

In a space where people
turn their bodies into bombs
rather than have their tongues
ripped asunder,
your depression
is inappropriate.
When the Israeli army
uses foreign journalists
as target practice
to further a media whiteout,
your depression
is inappropriate.

When children protect their homes
against tanks,
armed only with rocks
and righteous rage,
your depression

at a time like this
is inappropriate.

Toni Cade Bambara
said
>   *Depression*
>   *is collaboration*
>   *with the enemy.*
Then again,
you never have decided
which side you're on.
You better choose now
because as you keep telling me,
we are at war.
We are at war
with terrorism.
Translation:
Islam
brown people
justice
self-determination
freedom
dissent
and don't forget about that War on Drugs.
Yeah,
we're close to winning that one soon.
Bring our boys home
from slum streets and ghetto Gaza strips
where children are
armed with rocks and glocks
and misdirected righteous rage.

Double speak is the word of the day
obscuring the difference
between martyr
and murderer.

We didn't come here to kill
We came to die.
Whispers of Lolita Lebron
for we are the already dead
slaughtered child soldiers
bullet-ridden refugees
tortured freedom fighters.
We refuse to lie silent
in our mass unmarked graves
hidden from the harsh light of history.

Trust us,
they say.
Give history to us,
they say.
Give history to our blood-stained hands
and we will purify it,
burn it clean with our bleach.
It's a simple procedure, really:
Deny the creation
and you deny the occupation.
Deny the existence
and the resistance.
Deny the innocent who died
and you deny the genocide.
Deny the war games
Deny the family names -
they were too difficult for newscasters
to pronounce anyway.

Most of all,
deny the guns branded
U
S
A.

If you can't deny,
never forget the pass word
catch word
code words
military targets
we only bomb military targets

A blip on the screen
the beat of a heart
the cry of a child
the slip of a trigger
the push of a button
the slip of a dollar
can melt a 10-year-old's decapitated body
lying in the rubble
of a ruptured hospital
into

a military target.

These Are Not Safe Times to Love

Tender kisses are suspect
warm embraces
can be searched
for contraband.
We live under guard towers
heart-seeking missiles
aimed and ready.
Children run
arms flung wide
to embrace
battered bombs.

Packaged shelved
vacu-sealed emotions
mass produced attraction.
People pass each other
afraid of brushing against
the yawning pain
we have all become
walking around
on two legs.
Slide in between
two legs
sipping deeply
from
Lethe.
Forget the bruises
the silence
the anger

Forget my name
come first light.

No,
these
are not safe times to love
at all.

I wound myself
up
so tightly
I could not be unraveled.
Hid in the folds
of my flesh
away from the knowledge
that my heart
had slowed its beating.

It is the only way
I told myself
this crashing of bone and skin
this tidal wave of body
breaking over me in waves.

I always keep
my head
above water.

Then you slipped into my chest
reached out a hand
caressed my heart.
It had been so long
I forgot the taste of
this
this essence
newborn and tangy
sweat pooling in reservoirs
on supple backs.
            STOP THAT

The watchful guard tower booms
> *That is not permitted*
> *not permitted here*
> *where hands claw and grasp*
> *rather than encircle and uplift.*
> *That is not permitted*
> *not permitted here.*
> *We will have order*
> *and this*
> *is out of order.*

Fugitive acts
Rushing into love
a fugitive act
embracing it wide armed
full-lipped.

This easy
long-legged
tattooed
fingers-laced
Love.

Wings unfurled
skim the song
of sunrise.

Are you afraid
of flying
or falling?

The air rushing past my cheeks
feels like
your lips whispering kisses.
My ears fill
with the sound of your breath.

The earth below
is your broad sun face
moving beneath me.

As Icarus plummeted,
melted wax tears
and broken white wings
trailing in his wake,
did he regret
breaking through the sky?

I would not stop this rage of rapture
if I could.
Riding the currents of the heavens
is like
riding atop you.

These are not safe times to love
These are the only times to love.

Spring Blossoms

Spray-painted
on the last undetonated
atomic weapon
the cracked cityscape
broken eggshells
around the wound it dug:

> *STILL in the Shadow of steel barrs*
> *Some floWers are Stubborn enuf*
> *to grOw*
> *amidst the RUMBLE*
> ***Of bomBed decae***

Coffee and No Cigarettes

For Honky Tonk Man

You wake up at 5:30 in the morning
sky sucked clean of stars.
Drag your body into clothes,
into a borrowed car.
You drive two and a half hours until
you near White Deer, PA,
your gas station
french vanilla cappuccino
squirted out at 6:45 am
from the Hickory Run Plaza rest stop machine.
You turn off 1-80 W onto 15 N
at the
Snake Reptile House
exit.

Left at the wood carved sign
        United States Penitentiary Allenwood.
The speed limit is posted at 35 mph;
you drive 20.

Into the sterilized
processing center,
sign the book -
prisoner's name:
Clark Squire.
Slave names only.
It does not matter
how many decades
someone has been called
Sundiata Acoli
only slave names permitted here.

The visiting room
cold as a storage freezer.
Voices echo hollowly
above a murmur.
White plastic chairs
remind you of summer picnics.
But the only food to be had
comes out of
the wall of vending machines.
From these
you will drink countless cups
of french vanilla cappuccino.

The only time you drink coffee
is behind the walls of a prison.

Watch the families
around you,
waiting.
Watch the sun rise
on faces
as their loved one enters.
Hugs and long stolen kisses
under harsh fluorescent lights,
harsher eyes of guards
who must count in their heads
"One one thousand
two one thousand
three one thousand--
All right, break it up."

Finally
the door opens
and Sundiata walks out,
all 5'7 of him
(which he believes to be 5'9).

His face stern
his eyes drink in the room
in a second,
who is there,
table layout,
the guards' positions.
Every day survival.

His eyes fall on you,
his wide welcome home smile
splits his face,
a watermelon chopped open
on a hot summer day.

His brilliant mind
and no nonsense attitude
can be brusque,
you have learned.
But you have always
appreciated
people
who speak truth
without malice,
who speak love
without bullshit.

In between conversations,
men out on visits
come over to your table,
exchange greetings with Sundiata.
Older brothas with kufis
grey flecks in their beards
say
"Peace, brotha."
Tattooed stone-faced
young bucks

say
"Whassup, oldhead?"
and they mean it
as a sign of respect.
Once a prisoner
tall and rough hewn
with arms of granite and ghetto
came over
almost shyly
held out
a peanut butter Tasky Kake
to Sundiata,
rumbled,
"My girl got these for me
and I know you kinda feel them."
Smiled
ambled back to his assigned table.

Sundiata asks for report backs
information
ideas thoughts
experiences.
You bring him back
anything you touched
felt
saw
The beaches of Puerto Rico
The grave of Albizu Campos.
Second hand tales
of the jungles of Chiapas
and the struggles for land and dignity.
Second hand tales of the dusty roads
of Palestine
lined with bulldozers
and the struggle for land and dignity.

You listen
spellbound
to his tales
of life in rural Black Texas
life as a NASA mathematician
life in the Black Panther Party.
He does not tell many tales
of life in prison.
He tries to keep these visits
away from brutal beatings
and cold midnight cell bunks.
You know he worries
about your emotional well-being.
You shed tears
for this.

Sundiata's mind,
normally a steel trap,
begins to pull in different directions
as the tobacco withdrawal
grabs ahold of him.
He says,
"Aw shit,
the nicotine's got me again"
when he loses his train of thought
for the third time in an hour.
He cannot go out
grab a couple of puffs.
That is not allowed;
the visit
would be terminated.
He wants to quit,
but he has been smoking
half a century
and prison is no place
to quit smoking.

Your conversation
meandering before
speeds up
as you hurry
to get everything in
before visiting ends.

He'll tell you
you're getting too skinny
every visit.
He will tell you
Drive slowly
every visit.
You know
he will call you later that evening
to make sure you got home safe
every visit.

He will remind you
of a father
every single visit.

A visit
Is an entire universe unto itself
crushed and compressed
until it fits
into a plastic chair.

Even the universe must end.

A time of hurried goodbyes
of cleaning up the trash
to have something
to do with your hands.
The time of
I love yous

thank you for comings
I'll be back soons
multiplied
forty times
through the visiting room
as the collective unraveling
begins.

You give a hug
then the guard is at your elbow
herding you
towards the door.
Sundiata flashes you
his sun smile
and a raised Black fist
before the door slides open,
swallows him
whole.

All that is left:
return locker key
grab ID
get in the car.

At the stop sign before you clear
prison grounds,
you glance left
see four deer
two of them newborn fawns
still shaky in the legs.

See the sheen
of their coats,
moist noses.
Limpid trusting eyes
stare back at you

twenty feet away
from
concertina wire.

During processing,
a guard
said
they had to pull a deer
off the barbed wire
two days before.
It had gotten caught
and struggled
until it flayed itself open.

The guard shook his head:
"Dumb deer.
They're too stupid to know
they don't belong
here."

Prophet

Today I met a prophet
getting off the Q train
the smell of piss and pot smoke
succulent
heavy.
My heart was torn and swollen.
Today I needed a miracle
to make it through.

For so long
I have had no religion
save the love
we were able to steal.

His laughter cackled crackled
punctuated scriptures
pierced my self-righteous disbelief
in anything more judgmental
than myself.

Crucified in New York
stoned in South Central
shot 41 times in Jerusalem.
The only things
I held sacred
the laughter of children
the bellow of rebellion
your body
        moving beneath my hands
sweet sacrament.

My temple obliterated
scorched to the ground.
Our stolen love

ran dry
like god's forgiveness
like Palestinian children's tears.

I am drowning in this flood
sent to purify.

It was we who bled
in
Vieques
Tiananmen
Spanish Harlem
my bedroom.

I was left hanging
from your
barbed wire cross.

Detonate

My hand
dismantled
>The span of a 9mm
readied
>>Lock and load
Pistols growing out of severed
>*click*
Arm stumps
>*attention*
>Grenade where a heart should be
>>Aim
>>*and*

8.31.06

For the rebel spirit of Hasan Shakur

I.
No stay
There was no stay
We can't stay
here

II.
Where is Ossie
and why did he have to leave us
because we need
a eulogy
for another
shining
Black prince

III.
29
years
old
Too young
to be an ancestor
Too old
for this world

"He's gone onto a better place"
said the bearded white man
at the candlelight vigil
outside of the prison

FUCK YOU

IV.
107 degrees
Black crayon melts
The words burn up
Oh fuck
Hasan
burned up
We lost again
didn't we

In the car
outside the funeral home
where they're going
to burn
him up

    Don't cry
Hasan commanded

This is your show
so I'm sitting in this car
all the windows rolled up
sweating instead of sobbing
writing furiously
with a melting black crayon
trying to anchor you
so you can't leave
Staring at 11
bright-as-your-blood
mesh bags
all your worldly possessions
    What does crying get you
      waste of time
You never had
no time
to waste

It's 6:45 pm
At 5:58 we still had hope
At 6:07 the bottom
dropped
out of the universe
At 6:18 the press filed out
We knew
we had lost
this battle

The battle for you

I am wounded
my heart trailing
blood bright as those mesh bags
I try alchemy
anguish to anger
sobs to screams
I rage at their brutality
Vultures
tearing at all Black flesh
never sated

V.
But even in my suffering
I know this is not
a victory
for them

Today
the first and the last
time I saw you
you stared at me
with world worn child eyes
and promised
        Watch what I'm gonna do

Whether they kill me or not
watch what I'm gonna do
Ima make the ancestors proud

If I had not been
so arrogantly sure
there was still
room for justice in this world
I would have painted
the bulletproof glass
with Adinkra symbols
Akofena
        swords of war
Hye Wonhye
        that which cannot be burnt
Nsoromma
        child of the heavens

Whispered moans
like
Orisha prayers
Sung
through the cold buzzing phone

VI.
        Tell my people
        we must continue on
  Straps tighten
        Do not give up the fight
Cold metal bites flesh
        Do not give up hope
Needle against vein
        We can make it happen
Eyes on his wife's face

VII.
"Everyone has to leave
this world
one way"
the wise sistasage intoned
"You leave in your sleep
or strapped down
on their gurney
but you leave

The joke's on them
Though:
we all know
when a warrior
dies in battle
their spirit
continues the fight

If they thought
Hasan
was dangerous before
they have no idea
what he can do
let loose of the shackles of flesh
joined with all the ancestors
named and unnamed
unleashed
a furious storm
a ferocious wind
the blood in your arm
singing in your ears
telling you
we can do this
He's in the whirlwind
now
and if they thought

he was trouble
before

Just wait"

VIII.
I wish
I coulda
written
you free
but words
are no good
for getting free

The downpour
from my eyes
finally falls
like bodies
But I promise you
Hasan
I will not waste this

IX.
I will honor
you
with tears
used to oil
guns
the only eulogy
you asked for

Minefields II

under broken street lights
and infrared spot lights
at least
i exist
tangible
touchable
heavier than a nuclear bomb

i did not realize
i had let my dreams
die
radiation poisoning
until I heard your voice
singing
in my sleep
        sometimes i feel
        just like a motherless child
           a long
               way
                   from
and woke
in the middle of a minefield
laughing
with stars
in my hair

Prayer for Assata

Assata
Face wiped clean of age
Cheekbones you could fall off of
Body that flows like water over worn rocks
Dreadlocks splayed out and open
Trailing the scent of soothing aloe and sage

I wish Assata
Many beautiful lovers
Lovers who smell
Of earth
Warmed by the sun
Rather than despair that stinks
Like urine-stained tenement halls

She has known love
On the run
As sweetly intense
And dangerously fragile
As life at the barrel of a gun

Kiss twin scars directly beneath
Her breasts
Where two bullets
Are nestled still
Sleeping infants

I wish her lovers
With mango pulp between their teeth
And grape-stained hands
That soak into her

A lover with Shango in the hips
And the other Orishas under the tongue

Their love fried *platanos* for breakfast,
And freshly cut coconut before bed

Cat-eyes
Lean over her body
As hands move
Reading signs and songs
Etched in bark and cloth and skin
Praying
Dancing
Worshipping
The length of her arms
The heft of her flesh

Cowry shells pressed hot
Between two bodies
With ancient souls

I wish Assata
Someone who lets her be
Simply solely wholly
Assata
Comrade mother neighbor
That strong-limbed sista
Who can sure move those thighs
At a house party
Not a face on a wanted poster
Public enemy number one
Joanne Chesimard
Dead or alive
Two million dollar bounty on her head
To this day

Thunderstorms
Beat palm trees
And peel Che Guevara posters

Off the sides of Havana buildings
In the middle of the night
The screams of
Murdered
Stolen
Broken
Comrades pull back her dreads
To lick her neck
Tongues dripping defeat
Until they deafen her

But silence scars as well
Wounds left by over two years
Of solitary confinement
Of only hate-filled guards
Days when she forgot what a kind word was
She almost forgot she could speak
The wounds of silence
Can cut deeper than a machete
Cane stalks bleeding
Sugar blood

In prison
Fugitive love saved them
They were slaves
Catching a taste of sweetness
Bore fruit ripe and swollen
        This child
Of hope and wings
Of water and wind
Of thundering bars
And stinging darkness
Let us caress
Freedom's face
        Kiss deeply
        Full lips

Let us be human
For an hour
For these snatched seconds
Let us remember
What we look like in loving eyes

Let Assata always
Now look
Into loving eyes

Sky's the Limit

The unfinished revolution
Borne of the streets
Blood pours down the concrete
In turn
Birthing tracks in a studio
Laid down on wax.

Manifesting tell-tell stories,
Duplicating and recreating
The entire color spectrum.

Visions of the Brown Berets
Haunted by the CIA,
Undulating
Vibrating
Penetrating
The beat masturbating to itself
And in turn inseminating
Segments of the population.
Vietcong guerrilla fighting style,
Staggering through a mind field
Caught unawares.
Kamikaze situations
Night falls
Belly crawls through the tall grass.

Looped it with an SP 1200
Like the Ho Chi Minh trail.
Clearing out the stale empty posturings
Of this almost lost
Or perhaps a lost and found generation
Turn the station and find static.
The television spews me back at myself
In stereo surround sound

Surrounded
Fast closing in
Hit the dirt or assume the position,
Makes no difference.

Do not attempt to control us
We are in control of the control
Ciphering with the speed of a raised fist
Like this was the 68 Olympics.

And we're bombing cities
And bombing buildings
Spraypaint A-bombs
Twist off the top
Never stopped
To read the handwriting on the wall?
With blood in my eye
George Jackson resurrected
But to be corrected
By the department of corrections
Is akin to being overruled
By empty objections.
Cause for pause
Being Mumia Abu-Jamal
Still sitting in a cell.

Who volunteers
For a trip to the jungles of Chiapas?
The print of the Zapatistas mark me
And with sully on my forehead
I can't hope to stop this.

Increase the insurrection
Attica Attica
Turntables spin
With the prestige of a Mack 10

More or less deadly
We become the repository
For chains left
Unbroken.

The beat drops
The mic slinks through these streets
Twisting around this nation's larynx
Sanity cracks
Strange fruit
Hanging from Detroit lampposts
Hypercrossed like stars
A load too heavy to be laid down
Drowns out the silent screams of
Burning Buddhist monks
Revolutionaries shot dead while they slept
Children who've never wept.

Thanks to modern tricknology,
They are mass marketed
Circumcised and commodified
For a larger audience.

Bebop is lost
Crap rap is king
And emcees talk about
        Ayo, I rock the mic like Malik el-Shabazz
        Dropping bombs like this was Vietnam
But do you really?

You might
        Rock the mic like Fidel Castrooooooooo
But if you a counterrevolutionary
Then COINTELPRO incineraries
Got Castro
Rolling over in his soon-to-be grave.

Fuck the DAT machine
Che Guevara stalking through the hills.
Without making moves
Movement is lost
As are you.

Culture vultures perch on warheads
Waiting to drop something
On your head
And you talk about
How this mic is sacred
Then you desecrate and defecate
On the holy shrine of our ancestors
Talking bout
>   *Straight from the hip*
>   *Or the shoulder*
But when Huey Newton slipped
Who caught him?
Uncle Sam
With arms wide open.

Burrowing down into
The belly of the beast
Underground
Ripping from the inside out
Until I can breathe
Finally understanding
The powers that be
Are terrified
Because
WE BE THE POWER

If I play this track backwards
Voices scream for more than
Apple pie
Or a cabin in the sky

But I decide to just
Let
It
Drop.
And the record is not over yet
The record is not over yet
The revolution
Is not
Over
Yet.

Cartwheels in Prison Yards

For Haramia KiNassor

8 hours before
he was scheduled to depart this earth
8 hours before
hope slipped away
it was rekindled
wild brush forest fire

we
his wife and I
ran into the prison
whooping
screaming and singing
his father laughed through tears
his grandfather just nodded
he had never lost the faith

supporters with signs meant to shame a nation
did cartwheels across the green grass
tended by captive hands
I would have joined them
if I knew how to cartwheel

instead I flung my body down
buried my face in an earth
that still understood some semblance of justice
spread my arms wide
and took up space

we reclaimed the prison that day
for once there were no shouts of
        move along don't loiter
no hands on guns

no eyes narrowed
with hate and disdain
they knew we had won
and we were allowed this
our victory feast

even though they executed a man
the day before
even though they executed a man
the day after
every day that week
another candle extinguished
between fingers dipped in red

but on the fifth day they didn't rest
on the fifth day
we pushed them back
we roared their hands away from the switch
we knocked the needle out of his veins
with the blood pumping in ours
we broke restraints and twisted bars

we know it is not the end
but on the fifth day
8 hours before his execution
I did a somersault on the lawn of a prison
steeped in death

and smelled only the wild poppies

Frankenstein's Last Words

and regardless

of

everything

love

survives.

Thank Yous

My adopted brother Kakamia Jahad Imarisha, who has the incredible ability to turn a prison visiting room into a home, who paints raw and real with his words and his brush, who has shown me what unconditional love means.

Sundiata Acoli, whose sun smile warms me, educates me, recommits me constantly, even across a continent.

My godchildren Elijah and EKela, who have always been, since their births, the kind of people who make this world a beautiful place.

Turiya, my Good Sista, who created poetry and family with me, and who has shaped me as an artist and a human being.

Bayla, without whose constant presence in my life, I honestly would not be here.

My sister Jean, whose strength has always given me something to aspire to. To my sister Wanda (RIP). To all my family for helping me become the person I am.

Hasan Shakur (Rest in Power), whose commitment and determination will never be forgotten.

Haramia KiNassor, who taught me you can create beauty anywhere, even in the belly of hell.

Mumia Abu-Jamal, whose melodic insightful voice led me to political struggle and has guided me my entire adult life.

David Gilbert, who is truly the sweetest brilliant radical I have ever met. Free em all!

All of the innovative, fearless, visionary organizers, revolutionaries, rebels and artists I know (and don't know) locked behind walls.

My advisor (and friend) Matthew Shenoda, a brilliant mind and a poetic fighter.

Larry Colton, who has been my mentor for over a decade and a half, even if he won't admit it.

David Walker, who served as my North Star, keeping me moving in the right direction.

A single poem is the work of an entire community. Thank you to my visionary community, the artists and organizers who have inspired, challenged and sustained me (forgiveness and love to those I miss with this list but not with my heart) – Much love to Gabriel Teodros (thank you for your guidance on this book and the strength and boldness of your heart), Vagabond (thank you for everything, not the least of which the beautiful cover design!), Joseph (and Mary, RIP), DJ Ian Head, Seth Mulliken, Lil Pete, adrienne maree brown and all of *Octavia's Brood*, Nadia Maiwandi, Kent Ford and Patrice Lumumba Ford, Dr. Pastor Haynes, Climbing Poetree, Alexis Pauline Gumbs, Dr. Darrell Millner, Ariel Valenzuela, Rivas and Alegre, Fred Bryant, Bryonn Bain, Sham-e-ali, Jordan Flaherty, Ashanti Alston, Bao Phi, Avel Gordly, Dan Berger, Mark Gonzales, Claude Marks and Freedom Archives, Duiji MShinda, Blacque Butterfly, Rochell Rodeezy Hart, Mario Hardy, Dan Shea, Sam Chesneau, Mic Crenshaw and Jana Losey and Miss Audrey Love, Noah Prince, Mo Fee, Boots Riley and the Coup, Max Rameau and Take Back the Land, Toni Hill, Hasan Salaam, Oregon Universal Zulu Nation, Malik Delgado, Luke Querner, Addisalem and my beautiful South African conference peoples, Vursatyl and Jumbo from Lifesavas, Hari Kondabolu, Rolando and Sindy Avila, Jaime Guzman and Student Alliance Project/Papers/Oregon Dreamers, Terry Bisson, Dennis Gutierrez Zeledon, Aishah Shahidah Simmons, Kristian Williams, eL Seed, Moe Mitchell, Steve Elliott, Patricia Busbee, Roger Bonair-Agard, Staceyann Chin, Moe Mitchell, Lorenzo Komboa Ervin, Leah Lakshmi, Invincible, Jason Aragon and Pan Left, Jelani Wilson, Chris Jackson, Olmeca, Carlos Andres Gomez, OG One, March 4th,

Ahjamu Umi and the Black Working Group, tash shatz, Jabari Anderson, Fayemi Shakur, Ham'Diya Mu, The Human Rights Coalition, Jeff Chang, Sista Marpessa, Warsan Shire, Seattle Ladies First Collective, Steve Morozumi, NaTanya Davina Stewart, Withlove Felicia, Favianna Rodriguez and Culture Strike, Julio Salgado and Jesus Inigez and Dreamers Adrift, Azul and Cesar and Xloi and Oriana and the whole BMC Crew (where I was reborn), Leandra and Onna-lisa and Lisa and Michelle and Jacob and Paris and the VFE crew, Jeremy Glick, Camilo Mejia and Iraq Veterans Against the War, Sharon and Mariotta Gary-Smith, JinnOu, Marlena, Ricanstruction crew, Decolonize PDX, my APOC peoples, my Left Turn Magazine peoples, Al Letson, Alex Riedlinger, Alvaro Reyes, Amara Perez, Stephan Herrera, Daniel Hunter, Anh Phan, Kodey Park Bambino, Jessica Lee, John Joo and Standing Together/Our Families, Khalil and Antoinette Edwards, Ari Wohlfeiler, Eric Ward, and everyone who has shaped my life, my work, my art, my heart.

Author Bio

Photo by Pete Shaw

A historian at heart, reporter by (w)right, rebel by reason, Walidah Imarisha is an educator, writer, sci fi scholar, organizer and spoken word artist. Walidah was an editor of the first 9/11 anthology *Another World is Possible,* founding editor of *AWOL Magazine*, and served as Culture Editor for *Left Turn Magazine*. She is the co-editor of the upcoming anthology *Octavia's Brood: Science Fiction Stories From Social Justice Movements.*

One half of the poetry duo Good Sista/Bad Sista, Walidah's work has appeared in *Total Chaos: The Art And Aesthetics of Hip Hop, Letters From Young Activists, Daddy Can I Tell You Something, Word Warriors, The Quotable Rebel, Punk Rock Warlord: The Life and Work of Joe Strummer,* and *Life During Wartime: Resisting Counterinsurgency.*

She has taught in Portland State University's Black Studies Department, Oregon State University's Women, Gender and Sexuality Studies Department and Southern New Hampshire University's English and Literature Departments.

Made in the USA
San Bernardino, CA
26 January 2014